Knit-A-Block C[...]

Everything you need is here to make your own 'Blankets of Love'... for your family, for a friend, or to cheer someone special.

We included instructions for over 60 blocks to knit, crochet and quilt.

To begin, use the basic knit blocks on pages 6 - 7. Then add new designs for squares, or perhaps you'll want to invent new blocks.

Everyone can enjoy making these beautiful quilts and afghans.

Knit with Fabric Strips
Combined with Quilt Squares
page 4 - 5

Knit with Yarn
Combined with Quilt Squares
page 6 - 7

Knit-A-Block Afghans

Goldenrod
Knit and Crochet with Yarn
pages 20 - 21

Nature's Garden
Knit and Crochet with Yarn
pages 22 - 23

Red, White and Bold
Knit and Crochet with Yarn
pages 24 - 25

Spirits of the Earth
Knit and Crochet with Yarn
pages 26 - 27

Basic Supplies

Yarn or 1/4" wide fabric strips
Knitting needles size #10
Optional: Crochet hook

Index

'Layer Cake' Quilt

Fabric Blocks and Blocks Knit with Fabric

designed by Suzanne McNeill

I love fabric... I love to knit... and I love quilts, so I mixed and matched all three in these colorful quilts. What a wonderful combination of textures and colors! I assembled 10" x 10" blocks of colors... some knit and some fabric to make these quilted blankets.
You'll love the cozy feel of these beautiful quilts.

Basic Supplies: Cut and roll 1/4" wide strips into balls, and size #10 knitting needles.

Cut strips crosswise, alternately leaving 1/4" attached at **each selvage** edge. TIP: See page 18 to cut continuous strips.

After you knit, the squares will probably curl on the edges.

Flatten squares by pressing with a hot iron and a wet cloth until flat.

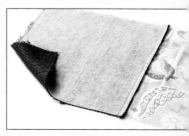

Stabilize knit blocks with lightweight iron-on interfacing on the back. With right sides together, sew knit and fabric blocks together.

Layer Cake Quilts

FINISHED SIZE: 47 1/2" x 66 1/2"

MATERIALS FOR KNITTING:

Top 7 colors of cotton fabric
    (1/4 yard each - cut into 1/4" wide strips)
Knitting needles, size #10

MATERIALS FOR COMPLETING THE QUILT:

Top 17 squares of 10" x 10" cotton fabric
    We used 1 'Layer Cake' of *Moda*
    "*Portugal*" fabric to make both quilts
Backing: 3 yards
Border #1   1/4 yard of 42" wide fabric
Border #2 & Binding 2 1/4 yards of 42" wide fabric
Batting: 50" x 80"
Needle and thread for sewing and quilting

SORTING:

Cut and set aside the following 10" x 10" squares:
Yellow & Red Quilt: 2 Red, 3 Blue, 3 Green
    and 7 knit blocks (3 Red - 4 Yellow)
Blue & Yellow Quilt: 2 Red, 3 Blue, 3 Green
    and 7 knit blocks (3 Green - 4 Blue)
From remaining 10" x 10" squares (both quilts):
    Cut 16 pieces 5" x 10".
    Cut 4 corner squares 5" x 5".
Refer to Assembly Diagram & photo for placement.

	Border		
Row 1			
Row 2		Knit Block	
Row 3	Knit Block		Knit Block
Row 4		Knit Block	
Row 5	Knit Block		Knit Block
Row 6		Knit Block	
Row 7			
	Border		

ASSEMBLY:

Arrange all Blocks on a surface or table.
Sew Row 1 together. Press.
Sew each row (2-3-4-5-6-7) together. Press.
Sew all 7 rows together.

BORDERS

Border #1:
Cut 5 strips 1 1/2" x 42".
Sew strips together end to end.
    Cut 2 strips 1 1/2" x 57" for sides.
    Cut 2 strips 1 1/2" x 40" for top & bottom.
    Sew side borders to the quilt. Press.
    Sew top and bottom borders. Press.
Border #2:
    Cut 2 strips 4 1/2" x 59" for sides.
    Cut 2 strips 4 1/2" x 48" for top & bottom.
    Sew side borders.to the quilt. Press.
    Sew top and bottom borders. Press.

10" x 10" Knit Square   10" x 10" Fabric Square

Basic Knit Block with Fabric

I used only the Stockinette Stitch to knit the blocks in this quilt - this pattern uses only basic knit and purl stitches, so even a beginner can easily accomplish these. The blocks knit up quickly and create wonderful textures.

Basic Knit Blocks - Stockinette Stitch

Cotton fabric (1/4 yard for each block)
Size #10 knitting needles with fabric cut into 1/4" wide strips
    Cast on 40 stitches.
    Rows 1 & 2: Knit 1 row. Purl 1 row.
    Repeat these 2 rows until block measures 10".
    Bind off.
        (Optional: Size #13 knitting needles with
        fabric cut into 3/8" wide strips. Cast on 30.)

Yellow Quilt   Blue Quilt

FINISHING:

Quilting:
    Layer the top of quilt, batting and backing in a 'sandwich' (see page 18).
    Make a quilting stitch pattern in each fabric block and in each knit block.
Binding:
    Cut strips 2 1/2" wide. Sew together end to end to equal 238". Fold in half.
    With right sides together, sew raw edges of binding around the edge of the quilt, being sure to make a tucked turn at each corner.
    Turn the folded edge around to the back and stitch in place.

10" x 10" Knit Square   10" x 10" Fabric Square

Basic Knit Block with Fabric

I used only the Stockinette Stitch to knit the blocks in this quilt - this pattern uses only basic knit and purl stitches, so even a beginner can easily accomplish these. The blocks knit up quickly and create wonderful textures.

Basic Knit Blocks - Stockinette Stitch

Worsted weight yarn (1 skein makes about 2 blocks)

Size #10 knitting needles
    Cast on 40 stitches.
    Rows 1 & 2: Knit 1 row. Purl 1 row.
    Repeat these 2 rows until block measures 10".
    Bind off.

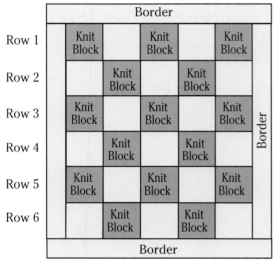

	Border				
Row 1	Knit Block		Knit Block		Knit Block
Row 2		Knit Block		Knit Block	
Row 3	Knit Block		Knit Block		Knit Block
Row 4		Knit Block		Knit Block	
Row 5	Knit Block		Knit Block		Knit Block
Row 6		Knit Block		Knit Block	
	Border				

(Border along right side)

Posh Patches Quilt

FINISHED SIZE: 57 1/2" x 67"

MATERIALS FOR KNITTING:

Top   8 skeins of worsted weight yarn:
      1 each of pink, orange, turquoise, dark
       green & purple - 2 each of royal blue
      (each skein makes about 2 blocks)

Knitting needles, size #10

MATERIALS FOR COMPLETING THE QUILT:

Top   17 squares of 10" x 10" cotton fabric
        We used 3 yards of *Moda* "Posh" fabric

Backing: 3 yards
Border & Binding   2 yards of 42" wide fabric
Batting: 66" x 75"

Needle and thread for sewing and quilting

ASSEMBLY:
    Arrange all Blocks on a surface or table.
    Sew row 1 together. Press.
    Sew each row (2-3-4-5-6) together. Press.
    Sew all 6 rows together. Press.

BORDER:
TIP: Cut the strips parallel to the selvage to eliminate piecing on the long borders.
    Cut 2 strips 5 1/2" x 57 1/2" for sides.
    Cut 2 strips 5 1/2" x 58" for top & bottom.
    Sew side borders to the quilt. Press.
    Sew top and bottom borders. Press.

FINISHING:

Quilting:
    Layer top of quilt, batting and backing in a 'sandwich' (see page 18).
    Make a quilting stitch pattern in each fabric block and in each knit block.

Binding:
    Cut strips 2 1/2" wide. Sew together end to end to equal 260". Fold in half.
    With right sides together, sew raw edges of binding around the edge of the quilt, being sure to make a tucked turn at each corner.
    Turn the folded edge around to the back and stitch in place.

Knit Blocks with Quilting

Posh Patches Quilt

Fabric Blocks and Blocks Knit with Yarn

designed by Suzanne McNeill

This beautiful patchwork quilt was sort of created by accident. I was experimenting with simple knit textures using some leftover yarn and made over a dozen blocks. I realized that to complete an afghan, I would need many more blocks and I was running out of time.

To speed up the process, I combined 10" x 10" squares of fabric with the yarn colors of knit blocks. My friend Julie Lawson came up with the idea to quilt all the blocks – fabric and yarn – for this versatile blanket.

Basic Supplies: Worsted weight yarn and Knitting needles size #10.

After you knit, the squares will probably curl on the edges.

Flatten squares by pressing with a hot iron and a wet cloth until flat.

Stabilize knit blocks with lightweight iron-on interfacing on the back. With right sides together, sew knit and fabric blocks together.

Basic Knit Blocks

You'll find all the basic blocks that I used to knit the quilts on these two pages. These squares use only basic knit and purl stitches, so even a beginner can accomplish these stitches.

Begin with Block 1 - the Stockinette Stitch. You can knit all the blocks with this stitch. As you become more confident, you may vary the stitches in the blocks to mix textures.

> **FOR ALL BLOCKS**
> Basic knitting instructions are on page 11.
> Worsted Weight Yarn • Size #10 needles
> about 8 stitches = 2"
> about 11 rows = 2"

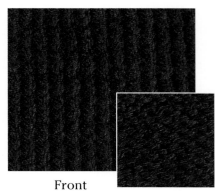

Front

Back

1 - Stockinette Stitch

Cast on 40 stitches.
Row 1: Knit 1 row.
Row 2: Purl 1 row.
Repeat these 2 rows until block measures 10".
Bind off.

2 - Garter Stitch

Cast on 40 stitches.
Knit every row until block measures 10".
Bind off.

3 - Wide Stripes

Cast on 39 stitches.
Row1: Knit 3, *Purl 3, Knit 3* Repeat * to *
Row2: Purl 3, *Knit 3, Purl 3* Repeat from * to *.
Repeat these 2 rows until block measures 10".
Bind off.

4 - Diamonds

Cast on 41 stitches.
Row 1: *Purl 1, Knit 9*, Repeat * to * ending Purl 1
Row 2: K 2, *P7, K3* Repeat * to * ending K2
Row 3: P3, *K5, P5* Repeat * to * ending P3
Row 4: K4, * P3, K7* Repeat * to * ending K4
Row 5: P 5, * K1, P9* Repeat * to * ending K5
Row 6: Repeat row 4
Row 7: Repeat row 3
Row 8: Repeat row 2
Repeat these 8 rows until block measures 10".
Bind off.

Front

Back

Front

Back

5 - Pebble Stripes

Cast on 40 stitches.
Rows 1 & 2: Knit 1 row. - Purl 1 row.
Rows 3 & 4: :K 1 row. - P 1 row.
Rows 5 & 6: :K 2 rows.
Repeat these 6 rows until block measures 10".
Bind off.

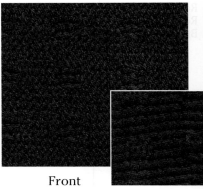

Front

Back

6 - Bubbles

Cast on 40 stitches.
Rows 1 & 2: Knit 1 row. - Purl 1 row.
Rows 3 & 4: K 1 row. - P 1 row.
Row 5: *K4, P4* Repeat across the row.
Row 6: *P4, K4* Repeat across the row.
Row 7: *K4, P4* Repeat across the row.
Row 8: *P4, K4* Repeat across the row.
Repeat these 8 rows until block measures 10".
Bind off.

7 - Half & Half

Cast on 40 stitches.
Row1: Knit Row2: Purl
Row3: Knit Row 4: Purl
Row 5: K1, P39 Row 6: K38, P2
Row 7: K3, P37 Row 8: K36, P4
Row 9: K5, P35 Row10: K34, P6
Row 11: K7, P 33 Row 12:K32, P8
Row13: K9,P31 Row 14: K30, P10
Row: 15 K11, P29 Row 16: K28, P12
Continue in this sequence increasing Ks on odd numbered rows by 2 and increasing Ps on even numbered rows by 2 until you have a diagonal division across the entire square.
Repeat rows 1 and 2 until block measures 10".
Bind off

Front

Back

8 - Columns

Cast on 40 stitches.
Row 1: Knit 1 row.
Row 2: Purl 1 row.
Row 3: K 1 row.
Row 4: P 1 row.
Row 5: *K2, P2* Repeat across the row.
Row 6: *P2, K2* Repeat across the row.
Row 7: *K2, P2* Repeat across the row.
Row 8: *P2, K2* Repeat across the row.
Repeat these 8 rows until block measures 10".
Bind off.

Front

Back

10 - Square in a Square

Cast on 40 stitches.
Row 1: Knit 1 row.
Row 2: Purl 1 row.
Rows 3 - 18: :Repeat these 2 rows for 3½".
Row 19: K15, P10, K15
Row 20: P15, K10, P15
Rows 21 - 38: Repeat these 2 rows for 3".
Row 39: K 1 row
Row 40: P 1 row
Rows 41 - 58: Repeat these 2 rows for 3½".
Repeat until the block measures 10"
Bind off.

12 - Checkerboard

Cast on 39 stitches.
Row 1: Knit 3, * Purl 3, Knit 3* Repeat * to *.
Row 2: Purl 3, *Knit 3, Purl3* Repeat * to *.
Row 3: Knit 3, *Purl 3, Knit 3* Repeat * to *.
Row: 4: Knit 3,*Purl 3, Knit 3* Repeat * to *.
Row 5: Purl 3,*Knit 3, Purl3* Repeat * to *.
Row 6: Knit 3, *Purl 3, Knit 3* Repeat * to *.
Row 7: Knit 3, * Purl 3, Knit 3* Repeat * to *
Row 8: Purl 3, *Knit 3, Purl 3* Repeat * to *.
Row 9: Knit 3, *Purl 3, Knit 3* Repeat * to *.
Repeat these 9 rows until block measures 10".
Bind off.

Front

Back

9 - Bumps

Cast on 40 stitches.
Row 1: Knit 1 row.
Row 2: Purl 1 row.
Row 3: K 1 row.
Row 4: *P4, K2* Repeat across row ending P4
Row 5: K 1 row.
Row 6: P 1 row.
Row 7: K 1 row.
Row8: P2, K2 *P4, K2* Repeat * to *
Repeat these 8 rows until block measures 10".
Bind off.

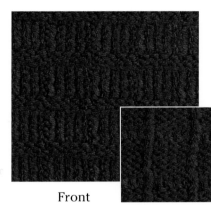

Front

Back

11 - Square to Square

Cast on 41 stitches.
Row 1: *P1, K 4* Repeat * to * ending P 1
Row 2: *K1, P4* Repeat * to * ending K1
Row 3: Repeat row 1
Row 4: Repeat row2
Row 5: Repeat row 1
Row 6: K one row
Row 7: P one row
Repeat these 7 rows until block measures 10".
Bind off.

Front

Back

13 - Heart of My Heart

Cast on 41 stitches.
Row 1: Purl Row2: Knit
Rows 3,4,5,6: Repeat Rows 1 and 2.

Row 7: P20,K1,P20.	Row 8: K20,P1,K20.
Row 9: P19,K3,P19	Row 10: K19,P3,K19.
Row 11: P18,K5,P18	Row 12: K18,P5,K18.
Row 13:P17,K7,P17	Row: 14 K17,P7,K17.
Row 15: P16,K9,P16	Row: 16 K16,P9,K16.
Row 17: P15,K11,P15	Row:18: K15,P11,K15.
Row 19: P14,K13,P14	Row: 20 K14,P13,K14.
Row 21: P13,K15,P13	Row 22: K13,P15,K13.
Row 23: P12,K17,P12	Row 24: K12,P17,K12.
Row 25: P11,K19,P11	Row 26: K11,P19,K11.
Row 27: P 10,K21,P10	Row 28: K10,P21,K10.
Row 29: P9,K23,P9	Row 30: K9,P23,K9.
Row 31: P8,K25,P8	Row 32: K8,P25,K8.
Row 33: P7,K27,P7	Row 34: K7,P27,K7.

Rows 35-40: Repeat rows 33 and 34.

Row 41: P9,K11,P1,K11,P9	Row 42: K9,P11,K1,P11,K9.
Row 43: P10,K9,P3,K9,P10	Row 44: K10,P9,K3,P9,K10.
Row 45: P11,K7,P5,K7,P11	Row 46: K11,P7,K5,P7,K11.
Row 47: P12,K5,P7,K5,P12	Row 48: K12,P5,K7,P5,K12.
Row 49: Purl one row.	Row 50: Knit one row.

Repeat rows 49 and 50 until block measures 10".
Bind off.

You'll love knitting
these blocks with only the
basic knitting stitches. You'll find more
variations on pages 11 through 18.

Healing...
One Step at a Time with 'Blankets of Love'

Southern California is an ideal place to live with mild winters and warm summers, but each year there is a fear of the "Santa Ana Winds." The hot dry winds arrive in September or October and last for three to five days at a time. Each season brings the fear of fire – fire from natural causes, fire from careless campfires in the hills or a careless match tossed from a moving car, and even a fire started by an arsonist.

In October of 2008, the Santa Ana winds were anticipated and predicted. The hot dry winds began and the threat of fire became a concern for the residents of the small town of Fallbrook. Fallbrook, the "Avocado Capital of the World," is nestled between San Diego to the south, San Bernardino to the north and Orange County to the west. The rolling hills of Fallbrook are interspersed with large and small avocado groves, citrus tree groves, small family estates, large custom built homes and small housing tracts. There is a great sense of community – of belonging and of caring for the citizens and families of Fallbrook.

The winds began and the events of the next seven days changed many lives. Shortly after midnight of the first day, about a third of the town was without power. The power lines had blown down causing the fire. By the end of the day, all residents were told by a reverse 911 telephone call to evacuate.

The fire had spread, closing off the two main highways in and out of town, and residents were told to leave through Camp Pendleton military base on a two-lane road. The sky grew black and the fire was spreading towards town. Each family started making the necessary plans to leave, where to meet loved ones, and what personal and necessary things to take in the limited space available.

Those people living in Valley Oaks Ranch were given 15 minutes to gather their belongings. Because it was a Monday, many were already at work, so they had absolutely nothing but the clothes on their backs. By the time the fire was over, 105 of their homes would be gone and the beautiful centuries-old oak trees would be burned stubs.

Our family was fortunate. My mother and her husband packed up their motorhome. My husband arrived home from work, and as a family, we decided what we would take with us – the two family pet rabbits, the children's toys and favorite stuffed animals, family pictures and a few treasured family gifts.

Along with the necessities, my aunt remembered to take her recipe box with her lifetime of collected favorite recipes.

As a family, we came from three ends of town to meet in the parking lot of a small mall to talk about how we would meet the challenge of the following days. A local grocery store helped us through the first meal by providing free the last of their barbequed chicken. All other stores, restaurants, and fast food places were forced to close by the fire department. We each made our way, very slowly, through the Camp Pendleton military base to Orange County.

My mother and her husband stayed at the State Park in their motorhome. The park was filled with residents and their belongings. Some brought their goats, horses, llamas, chickens, a parrot, dogs and cats. Each day local Orange County fast food restaurants and Starbucks brought warm food and coffee to share and people gathered in small friendship groups. My aunt and our family were fortunate to stay with my father, who had an old converted barn with very rustic accommodations.

The children comforted their bunnies (who now had their own portable cages) while the adults gathered around the television to observe the progress of the fires in Southern California. It seemed as though all of Southern California was aflame. Daily, a trip was made to the library to check out the Internet site listing the streets and home addresses that were on the "loss-of-home" list. Each day we felt blessed - the fire was close, very close, but our homes had not burned.

After several days, we returned to our homes, our community. The small town of Fallbrook lost over 200 homes. The town began the process of clean-up and healing. Appreciation was expressed for the tremendous efforts made by the fire departments that helped in our time of need. Fire teams came from all over California, from Oregon, and from Arizona. Each team brought 5 fire trucks and firemen to man them. There was a huge, well-organized and coordinated effort to house, feed, and give direction to the fire teams. Through their bravery and their fire fighting efforts, our communities were spared a greater loss.

In the next days and weeks we began to hear story after story of brave residents who stayed and helped save their neighbors' property. Each story was about people, family and friends. There was caring and sharing, from little acts of kindness to community and church support groups.

Everyone wanted to help – to give of their time and their talents to bring some comfort to others. It was at this time that the project of making "Blankets of Love" for the fire victims was initiated. As the owner of 'Labors of Love' in Fallbrook, I realized there was an opportunity to give back to the community and the people of Fallbrook who had lost their homes.

The people of Fallbrook were invited to help with the project. As the store owner, I gladly donated skeins of Vanna's Choice, Lion Brand Yarn to each participant. I also called Lion Brand Yarns in New York and asked if they would be willing to donate some yarn. Shortly thereafter, a box of yarn arrived to help with our project. What a welcome and appreciated surprise! Directions were given to the participants to create a square from the yarn.

More than 100 ladies and children participated in the project with some coming back many times to receive a new ball of yarn to make squares. Each participant had a wide selection of colors to choose from. In the end, stacks and stacks of squares were accumulated.

The squares were the creation of the knitter or crocheter, with some squares being very simple while others had very detailed patterns. My aunt graciously took the squares to her home. Together we laid out the colors and designs to create 26 beautiful blankets.

As each participant received or brought back their squares, we listened to their personal stories of the fire. Some of our customers lost their homes, some had family members or special friends that lost their homes.

A list was formed of those to whom we wanted to give a blanket. On Valentine's Day, the finished blankets were displayed in our 'Labors of Love' store. All of the participants and townspeople were invited to join in our celebration. Those who knew of someone who had lost a home were invited to pick up a blanket and deliver it to their friend or family member.

Pictures tell the story. Each one who received a blanket is recorded on film. The pictures capture the emotion of giving and receiving. In the end, the project was about thoughtfulness, giving, and caring. Our community is healing. Homes are being rebuilt. The fields are turning green and avocado groves are beginning to sprout new leaves.

The care and love that people have for one another following the fires continues to grow, and our families and friends have a sense of belonging far greater now than before the fires.

We believe that one stitch at a time we were able to heal our own hearts and, more importantly, the hearts of those who lost their homes and personal belongings.

Debra Riesenberg

Basic Crochet

Crochet blocks are simple and look great in every color. It is easy to combine crochet, knit and quilt blocks - as long as the finish size of the block is the same.

Basic Steps and Stitches
Refer to a book on crochet stitches for detailed instructions.

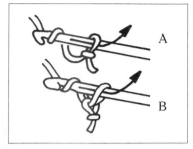

CHAIN STITCH (ch): Tie a slip knot in yarn ends. Insert hook through loop. Yarn over hook, pull through (A). Repeat for the desired number of chs (B).

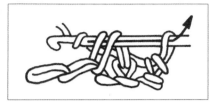

SLIP STITCH (sl): Insert hook in stitch. Yarn over hook, pull through stitch and loop on hook.

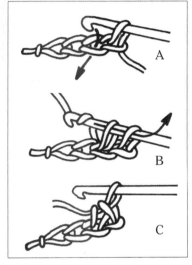

SINGLE CROCHET (sc): (A) Insert hook in second ch from hook. Yarn over hook, draw up a loop - 2 loops on hook. (B). Draw loop through both loops on hook. (C) Sc completed.

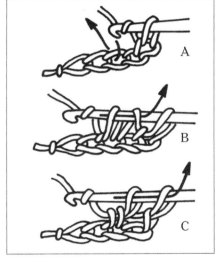

DOUBLE CROCHET (dc): (A) Yarn over hook, insert hook into 3rd chain from hook. Pull up a loop - 3 loops on hook. (B) Yarn over hook, draw loop through 2 loops. (C).Yarn over hook, pull through the last 2 loops on hook.

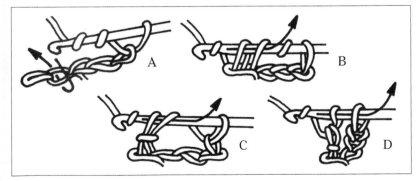

TRIPLE CROCHET (tc): (A) Yarn over hook twice, insert hook into the 4th chain from hook. (B) Yarn over hook, pull up a loop - 4 loops on hook. (C) Yarn over hook, draw through 2 loops - 3 loops on hook. (D) Yarn over hook, draw through the last 2 loops.

Basic Knitting

Basic stitches that I use to knit most of my squares include - knit and purl. Even a beginner can easily accomplish these stitches.

Knit all blocks with the basic Block 1 on page 8, or you can vary the stitches in the blocks to mix and match textures as you become more confident.

Basic Steps and Stitches
Refer to a book on knitting stitches for detailed instructions on how to knit.

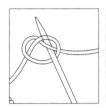 

CAST ON: 1. Begin with a row of foundation stitches worked each stitch onto one needle. Make a slip knot, leave a 4" tail, pull the stitch taut.

2. Add foundation stitches by using a second needle and your finger to loop thread into stitches.

3. Keep foundation stitches on one needle. Add as many as needed.

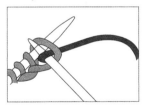 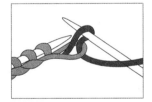

KNIT: Add each knit stitch with loops to the <u>front</u> thru the foundation stitches.

Slip each knit loop from the left needle to the right needle.

PURL: Add each stitch with loops to the <u>back</u>. Slip each purl loop to the right needle.

 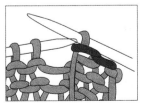

BIND OFF: End by binding off on the last row. On the last row, stitches are secured 'off the needle'.

Worsted weight yarn

(4 ply) is used for all projects.

---

for Knitting: Knitting needles size 10

Knit Symbols and Abreviations:

K	knit stitch
P	purl stitch
yo	yarn over (see page 17)

for Crochet : Crochet hook sizeJ/10 - 6mm

Crochet Symbols and Abreviations:

ch	chain
sl	slip stitch
sc	single crochet stitch
dc	double crochet stitch
tc	triple crochet stitch
sk	skip a stitch
yo	yarn over

---

14 - Triple Crochet
Rows of Crochet

Crochet:

Begin: Ch 35.

Row 1: Tc in 4th ch from hook. work tc in each chain stitch across the row. Ch 4. Turn.

Row 2: Tc in each stitch across. Ch. 4. Turn.

Repeat Row 2 until block measures 10".

15 - Granny Square '1'
Rounds of Crochet
Clusters of Double Crochet Stitches

Crochet:

Note: Use color 1 for rnds 1 & 2, color 2 for rnds 3 & 4 and color 3 for remaining rounds.

Begin: Ch 4, join with a sl st to form a ring.

Round 1:

Ch 3 (counts as 1 dc stitch).

Work 2 dc in center of ring. Work (*ch 2, 3 dc in ring).

Repeat from * two more times (for a total of 4 clusters). End with a ch 2, join with a sl st in 3rd st of chain.

Round 2:

Ch 3 (counts as 1 dc stitch). Turn.

Work 2 dc, ch 2, 3 dc - all in the ch-2 space of previous round (this is a corner). Work (*ch 1, now work 3 dc, ch 2, 3 dc) in next ch-2 space at the corner.*

Repeat from * twice for remaining corners. End with a ch 1, join with a sl st in 3rd st of chain.

Round 3:

Ch 3 (counts as 1 dc). Turn. Work 2 dc, ch 1 in next ch-1 space of previous row.

Work (*3 dc, ch 2, 3 dc) in the next ch-2 space of previous row.

Work (ch 1, 3 dc, ch 1) in each ch-1 space along the side and (3 dc, ch 2, 3 dc) in each ch-2 space for corners. Repeat from * ending ch 1. Join with a sl st in 3rd st of chain.

Repeat round 3 until block measures 10".

16 - Seed Stitch Diamonds
Rows of Knitting

Knit:

Cast on 39 stitches.

Row 1: K1, *(K3, P1) 2 times, K1, P1*. Repeat * to * ending K3, P1, K4.

Row 2: P1 *(P3, K1) 2 times, P1, K1*. Repeat * to * ending P3, K1, P4.

Row 3: K3, P1, K1, P1 *(K3, P1) 2 times, K1, P1*. Repeat * to * ending K3.

Row 4: P3, K1, P1, K1 *(P3, K1) 2 times, P1, K1*. Repeat * to * ending P3.

Row 5: K1, (K1, P1) 3 times *(K2, P1) 2 times, (K1, P1) 2 times*. Repeat * to * ending K2.

Row 6: P1, (P1, K1) 3 times, *(P2, K1) 2 times, (P1, K1) 2 times*. Repeat * to * ending P2.

Row 7: Repeat Row 3.

Row 8: Repeat Row 4.

Row 9: Repeat Row 1.

Row 10: Repeat Row 2.

Row 11: K4, P1, *K2 (P1, K1) 2 times, P1, K2, P1*. Repeat * to * ending K4.

Row 12: P4, K1, *P2, (K1, P1) 2 times, K1, P2, K1*. Repeat * to * ending P3.

Repeat Rows 1-12 until block is 10".

Bind off.

17 - Granny Square '2'
Rounds of Crochet

Crochet:

Note: Use color 1 for rnds 1,2 & 3, color 2 for rnds 4 & 5 and color 3 for remaining rounds.

Begin: Ch 4, join with sl st to form a ring.

Round 1:

Ch 3 (counts as a 1 dc).

Work 2 dc in the center of ring.

Work (*ch 2, 3 dc in ring).

Repeat from * two more times. End with a ch 2, join with a sl st in 3rd st of chain.

Round 2:

Ch 4 (counts as 1 dc & 1 ch). Skip 1 dc and work a dc in the next dc. Work (*2 dc, ch 2, 2 dc) in ch-2 of corner space. Work (dc in next dc, ch 1, skip 1 dc, dc in next dc) for sides.

Repeat from * two times.

Work (2 dc, ch 2, 2 dc) in the ch-2 of corner space. Join with a sl st in the 3rd st of chain.

Round 3:

Ch 3 (counts as 1 dc & 1 ch).

Work a dc in the next 3 dc.

Work (*2 dc, ch 2, 2 dc) in ch-2 of corner space. Work dc in the next 3 dc, ch 1, dc in next 3 dc.

Repeat from * two times.

Work (2 dc, ch 2, 2 dc) in corner, dc in the next 3 dc. Join with sl st in 3rd st of chain.

Additional Rounds:

Work in established pattern, increasing dcs on side rows until block measures 10".

18 - Twisted Rib
Rows of Knitting

Knit:

Cast on 40 stitches.

Row 1: Work (K1 into the back of the next st, P1) across.

Row 2: Work (Knit 1 into the back of each knit st, Purl each Purl st) across.

Repeat Rows 1 and 2 until block measures 10".

Bind off.

19 - Double Crochet
Rows of Crochet

Crochet:

Begin: Ch 34.

Row 1: Dc in 3rd ch from hook. work dc in each chain across the row. Ch 3. Turn.

Row 2: Dc in each stitch across the row. Ch 3. Turn.

Repeat Row 2 until block measures 10".

20 - Moss Ribbing
Rows of Knitting

Knit:

Cast on 40 stitches.

Make knot stitch as follows: Wrap yarn around needle, making a stitch. Pass the second stitch from the right needle over first stitch and the made stitch. To complete knot, wrap yarn around needle again and pass second stitch over the 2 made stitches.

Row 1: *K1 (P1, K1) 2 times, slip one stitch as if to purl, K1, slip one stitch as if to purl*. Repeat to end of row.

Row 2: *P3, (K1, P1) 2 times, K1*. Repeat until end of row.

Repeat Rows 1-2 until block measures 10".

Bind off.

21 - Triple and Single
Rows of Crochet

Crochet:

Begin: Ch 32.

Row 1: Sc in 2nd ch from hook. work sc in each chain across the row. Ch 4. Turn.

Row 2: Tc in each stitch across. Ch 2. Turn.

Row 3: Sc in each stitch across. Ch 4. Turn.

Repeat Rows 2 and 3 until block measures 10".

22 - Triple Crochet
Rows of Crochet

Crochet:

Begin: Ch 35.
Row 1: Tc in 4th ch from hook. work tc in each chain stitch across the row. Ch 4. Turn.
Row 2: Tc in each stitch across. Ch 4. Turn.
Repeat Row 2 until block measures 10".

23 - Stockinette Stitch with Homespun Yarn
Rows of Knitting

Knit:

Cast on 40 stitches.
Row 1: Knit 1 row
Row 2: Purl 1 row.
Repeat these 2 rows for 10".
Bind off.

see photos on page 21

Worsted weight yarn
for Knitting: Knitting needles size 10 or
for Crochet: Crochet hook size J/10 - 6mm

24 - Double Crochet
Rows of Crochet

Crochet:

Begin: Ch 34.
Row 1: Dc in 3th ch from hook. Work dc in each chain across the row. Ch 3. Turn.
Row 2: Dc in each stitch across. Ch 3. Turn.
Repeat Row 2 until block measures 10".

25 - Quaker Variation
Rows of Knitting

Knit:

Cast on 39 stitches.
Row 1: Purl.
Row 2: K1, *yarn forward slip 1 stitch as if to purl, K1*. Repeat * to * across row.
Repeat Rows 1 and 2 until block is 10".
Bind off.

26 - Seed Stitch
Rows of Knitting

Knit:

Cast on 41 stitches.
Work (K1, P1) across, ending K1.
Repeat this row until block is 10".
Bind off.

27 - Wide Welts
Rows of Knitting

Knit:

Cast on 40 stitches.
Rows 1-15: Work in stockinette stitch (K1 row, P1 row).
Rows 16-19: Knit.
Row 20: Purl.
Rows 21-35: Work in stockinette stitch.
Rows 36-39: Knit.
Row 40: Purl
Work remaining rows in stockinette stitch until block measures 10".
Bind off.

28 - Triple Crochet
Rows of Crochet

Crochet:

Begin: Ch 35.
Row 1: Tc in 4th ch from hook. Work tc in each chain stitch across the row. Ch 4. Turn.
Row 2: Tc in each stitch across. Ch 4. Turn.
Repeat Row 2 until block measures 10".

29 - Diamonds for You
Rows of Knitting

Knit:

Cast on 40 stitches.
Row 1: Work (P1, K7) across.
Rows 2 and 8: Work (K1, P5, K1, P1) across.
Rows 3 and 7: Work (K2, P1, K3, P1, K1) across.
Rows 4 and 6: Work (P2, K1, P1, K1, P3) across.
Row 5: Work (K4, P1, K3) across.
Repeat Rows 1-8 until block is 10".
Bind off.

30 - Granny Square '3'
Rounds of Crochet

Crochet:

Note: Use color 1 for rnd 1, color 2 for rnd 2, color 3 for rnd 3, color 4 for rnd 4, and color 5 for remaining rounds.

Work the rounds the same as for Granny Square '1' on page 12.

31 - Triple Sets
Rows of Crochet

Crochet:

Begin: Ch 33.
Row 1: Sc in 2nd ch from hook. Work sc in each chain across the row. Ch 3. Turn.
Row 2: Dc in each chain across. Ch 4. Turn.
Row 3: Tc in each stitch across. Ch 2. Turn.
Row 4: Sc in each stitch across. Ch 3. Turn.
Repeat Rows 2, 3 and 4 until block measures 10".

32 - Dancing Dots
Rows of Knitting

Knot Stitch:
(Bring yarn forward, wrap it over needle to the back, pass second stitch from right needle point over first stitch and made stitch.) 2 times

Cast on 40 stitches.
Row 1: *K2 (Knot st, K1) twice, Knot st*. Repeat * to * across row.
Row 2 and all even numbered rows: Purl.
Row 3: *K4, Knot st, K2, Knot st*. Repeat * to * across row.
Row 5: *K3, Knot st*. Repeat * to * across row.
Row 7: *K4, Knot st, K4*. Repeat * to * across row.
Row 9: *K2, Knot st, (K1, Knot st) twice*. Repeat * to * across row.
Repeat Rows 1-10 until block is 10".
Bind off.

33 - Welt Variation
Rows of Knitting

Knit:

Cast on 40 stitches.
Row 1: Knit.
Row 2: Purl.
Rows 3 and 4: Knit.
Row 5: Purl.
Row 6: Knit.
Repeat Rows 1-6 until block is 10".
Bind off.

34 - Variation Stitch
Rows of Knitting

Knit:

Cast on 41 stitches or any odd number of stitches necessary to achieve gauge. Work an equal number of added stitches at each end of each row in established pattern.

Row 1: Purl. (Wrong side)
Rows 2 and 3: Knit.
Rows 4-9: Repeat Rows 1-3 twice.
Row 10: Purl.
Row 11: Knit.
Row 12: Purl.
Row 13: Knit.
Row 14: Purl.
Row 15: K3, work (P5, K5) across, ending K3.
Row 16: P3, work (K5, P5) across, ending P3.
Rows 17-19: Repeat Rows 11-13.
Row 20: Repeat Row 16.
Row 21: Repeat Row 16.
Row 22: Purl.
Row 23: Knit.
Row 24: Purl.
Repeat Rows 23 and 24 until block is 10".
Bind off.

35 - Big Welt Stitch
Rows of Knitting

Knit:

Cast on 39 stitches.
Row 1: *P3, K3*. Repeat * to * across row ending P3.
Row 2: Knit.
Repeat Rows 1-2 until block is 10".
Bind off.

see photos on page 23

Worsted weight yarn
for Knitting: Knitting needles size 10 or
for Crochet: Crochet hook size J/10 - 6mm

36 - Granny Square '4'
Rounds of Crochet
Crochet:

Note: Use color 1 for rnd 1, color 2 for rnds 2, 3 & 4 and color 3 for remaining rounds.

Work the rounds the same as for Granny Square '1' on page 12.

37 - Granny Square '5'
Rounds of Crochet
Crochet:

Note: Use color 1 for rnd 1, color 2 for rnds 2, 3 & 4, color 3 for rnd 5, and color 4 for remaining rounds.

Begin: Ch 4, join with a sl st to form a ring.
Round 1: Ch 4 (counts as a tc).

Work 15 tc in the center of ring (for a total of 16 'rays'. Join with a sl st in the 4th stitch of chain. Ch 3. Turn.

continued

Round 2: Work 1 dc in the 1st st.

Work 2 dc in each of the next 3 stitches.

Work (*ch 3 for the corner, 2 dc in each of the next 4 stitches, ch 3 for another corner).

Repeat from * 2 more times. Join with a sl st in 3rd st of chain.
Round 3: Ch 3 (counts as dc), 3 dc, ch 2, 4 dc in corner.

Work (*ch 2, 2 dc in space after 4 dcs, ch 2. Work (4 dc, ch 2, 4 dc) in corner.

Repeat from * ending with a corner. Join with a sl st in the 3rd stitch of chain.
Round 4: Ch 3 (counts as a dc).

Work 3 dc, ch 2, 3 dc in the next ch-2 space of previous row - this is a corner.

Work (*ch 1, 3dc) in every ch-2 space along the side, ch 1, and (3 dc, ch 2, 3 dc) in the next ch-2 space at the corner.

Repeat from * around ending ch 1, 3 dc in space, ch 1, 2 dc in corner. Join with a sl st in the 3rd stitch of chain.

Repeat Round 3 until block measures 10".

38 - Big Ripple Stitch
Rows of Crochet
Crochet:

Begin: Ch 34.
Row 1: Work 1 sc in 2nd chain on hook. Work sc across the row. Ch 2. Turn.
Row 2: Work (*1 sc, 1 dc, 1 tc, 1 dc).

Repeat from * across the row, ending with 1 sc in the last st. Ch 4. Turn.
Row 3: Work (*1 tc, 1 dc, 1 sc, 1 dc, 1 tc).

Repeat from * across the row, ending with 1 tc in the last st. Ch 2. Turn.
Repeat Rows 2 & 3 until block measures 10".

39 - Granny Square '6'
Rounds of Crochet
Crochet:

Note: Use color 1 for rnds 1 & 2, color 2 for rnds 3, 4 & 5, color 3 for rnd 6, color 4 for rnd 7 and color 5 for remaining rounds.

Work the rounds the same as for Granny Square '1' on page 12.

40 - Framed Square
Rows of Crochet
Crochet:

Begin: Ch 34. Turn.
Row 1: Sc in 2nd chain from hook, sc in each ch across the row. Ch 2. Turn.
Row 2: Sc in each stitch across. Ch 2. Turn.
Row 3: Work (*sc 2, yo 1 and sk 1). Repeat from * across the row. End with sc 2. Ch 2. Turn.
NOTE: When you yo, it will make an extra loop on the next sc.
Row 4: Work (*sc in 1 stitch, 2 sc in yo stitch). Repeat from * across. End with 2 sc. Ch 2. Turn.
Row 5: Sc in the first 2 stitches, yo 1 and sk 1 stitch. sc in each stitch across to the last 3 stitches.

Work yo and sk 1 stitch, 2 sc. Ch 2. Turn.

Row 6: Sc in the first stitch. Work (*2 sc in yo stitch, sc in 1 stitch).

Repeat from * across the row, until the last 3 stitches. Work 2 sc in yo stitch. End with 2 sc. Ch 2. Turn.
Repeat Rows 5 & 6 until block measures 9".
Next Row: Repeat Row 3.
Last 2 Rows: Repeat Row 4. Repeat Row 2.

41 - Garter Ribs
Rows of Knitting

Knit:

Cast on 40 stitches.
Row 1: Knit.
Row 2: *K2, P2*. Repeat across row.
Repeat Rows 1 and 2 until block is 10".
Bind off.

42 - Shells
Rows of Crochet

Crochet:

Begin: Ch 34. Turn.
Row 1: Work sc in 3rd chain on the hook. Sc across the row. Ch 3. Turn.
Row 2: Work 1 dc in the 1st stitch. Work (*sk 1, 2 dc in the next st).

Repeat from * across the row, ending with 1 dc in the last st. Ch 3. Turn.
Repeat Row 2 until block measures 10".

43 - Granny Square '7'
Rounds of Crochet
Crochet:

Note: Use color 1 for rnd 1, color 2 for rnds 2 & 3, color 3 for rnds 4 & 5, color 4 for remaining rounds.

Work the rounds the same as for Granny Square '1' on page 12.

44 - Granny Square '8'
Rounds of Crochet
Crochet:

Note: Use one color for all rounds.

Work the rounds the same as for Granny Square '1' on page 12.

45 - Granny Square '9'
Rounds of Crochet
Crochet:

Note: Use color 1 for rnds 1 & 2, color 2 for rnds 3, 4 & 5, color 3 for rnd 6, color 4 for remaining rounds.

Work the rounds the same as for Granny Square '1' on page 12.

46 - Granny Square '10'
Rounds of Crochet
Crochet:

Note: Use one color for all rounds.

Work the rounds the same as for Granny Square '1' on page 12.

47 - Cluster Shells
Rows of Crochet
Crochet:

Begin: Ch 34. Turn.

Row 1: Work sc in 3rd chain on the hook. Sc across the row. Ch 3. Turn.
CLUSTER STITCH:
Work (*yo, insert hook in ring, yo and pull through 1 loop, yo and pull through 2 loops - keeping the last loop on the hook).
Row 2: Work a 'Cluster Stitch' in each stitch across the row. Ch 3. Turn.
Row 3: Work (*a 'Cluster Stitch', 1 sc).
Repeat from * across the row, ending with 1 sc in the last st. Ch. 3. Turn.
Repeat Row 3 until block measures 10".

see photos on page 24

Worsted weight yarn
for Knitting: Knitting needles size 10 or
for Crochet: Crochet hook size J/10 - 6mm

48 - Granny Square '11'
Rounds of Crochet
Crochet:

Note: Use color 1 for rnd 1, color 2 for rnds 2, 3 & 4, and color 3 for remaining rounds.
Work the rounds the same as for Granny Square '1' on page 12.

49 - Single Crochet
Rows of Crochet
Crochet:

Begin: Ch 32.
Row 1: Work sc in 2nd ch from hook. Sc in each chain across the row. Ch 3. Turn.
Row 2: Sc in each stitch across. Ch. 3. Turn.
Repeat Row 2 until block measures 10".

50 - Granny Square '12'
Rounds of Crochet
Crochet:

Note: Use color 1 for rnd 1, color 2 for rnd 2, color 3 for rnds 3 & 4, color 4 for rnd 5, and color 5 for remaining rounds.
Work the rounds the same as for Granny Square '1' on page 12.

51 - Giant Welts
Rows of Knitting
Knit:
Cast on 40 stitches.
Row 1: Knit.
Row 2: Purl.
Rows 3-6: Repeat Rows 1-2.
Row 7: Purl.
Row 8: Knit.
Rows 9-12: Repeat Rows 7-8.
Repeat Rows 1-12 until block is 10".
Bind off.

52 - Granny Square '13'
Rounds of Crochet
Crochet:

Note: Use color 1 for rnd 1, color 2 for rnd 2, color 3 for rnd 3, color 4 for remaining rounds.

Begin: Ch 4, join with a sl st to form a ring.
Round 1:
Ch 3 (counts as 1 dc).
Work 11 dc in ring (for a total of 12 'rays'). Join with a sl st in the 3rd stitch of ch.
Round 2:
Ch 3 (counts as 1 dc). Turn.
Work 2 dc in the first st, ch 1.
Work (*3 dc in each stitch, ch 1).
Repeat from * around. Join with a sl st in 3rd st of ch.
Round 3:
Ch 4 (counts as 1 tc). Turn.
Work 2 tc, ch 1 in a ch-1 space.
Work (*3 tc, ch 2, 3 tc in next ch-1 - this is a corner. Work 3 tc in next two ch-1 spaces).
Repeat from * around. End with a ch 1. Join with a sl st in the 3rd stitch of ch.
Round 4:
Ch 3 (counts as 1 dc stitch on rnd 4). Turn.
Work 2 dc, ch 2. In next ch-1 space, work 3 dc in the next ch-1 space of previous row.
Work (*ch 1, 3dc - in every ch-1 space along the side, ch 1), and (3 dc, ch 2, 3 dc) in the next ch-2 space - this is a corner.
Repeat from * around. End with a Ch 1. Join with a sl st in the 3rd stitch of ch.
Repeat Round 4 until block measures 10".

53 - Shells
Rows of Crochet
Crochet:

Begin: Ch 34. Turn.

Row 1: Work sc in 3rd chain on the hook. Sc across the row. Ch 3. Turn.
Row 2: Work 1 dc in the 1st stitch. Work (*sk 1, 2 dc in the next st).
Repeat from * across the row, ending with 1 dc in the last st. Ch. 3. Turn.
Repeat Row 2 until block measures 10".

54 - Granny Square '14'
Rounds of Crochet
Crochet:

Note: Use color 1 for rnds 1, 2 & 3, color 2 for rnds 4, 5 & 6, color 3 for rnd 7, color 4 for remaining rounds.

Begin: Ch 4, join with a sl st to form a ring.
Round 1: Ch 3 (counts as 1 dc).
Work 15 dc in ring (for a total of 16 'rays'). Join with a sl st in the 3rd stitch of chain.

continued

Round 2: Ch 4 (counts as dc + 1 ch).
Work dc in the space between the 1st and 2nd dc.
Work (*ch 1, skip 1 dc, dc in space between stitches). Repeat from * around the row, ending ch 1. Join with a sl st in the 3rd stitch of chain.

POPCORN STITCH:
Work (*yo, insert hook in ring, yo and pull through 1 loop, yo and pull through 2 loops, yo and pull through 3 loops - keeping the last loop on the hook).
Repeat from * 4 more times.
Yo and pull through the last 6 loops.)
Round 3: Ch 3 (counts as 1 dc).
Work (*a **popcorn stitch** in each ch-1 space from the previous row, ch 1).
Repeat from * around. Join with a sl st.
Round 4:
Ch 3 (counts as 1 dc stitch on rnd 3). Turn.
Work 1 dc, ch 1in the next ch-1 space.
Work (2 dc, ch 1) in each of the next 3 ch-1 spaces for the side, ch 1 .
Work 3 tc, ch 2, 3 tc in the next ch-1 sp - this is the corner, ch 1. Work (2 dc, ch 1) in each of the next 3 ch-1 spaces for the side. Ch 1.
Repeat from * around, ending with a corner, ch-1. Join with a sl st.
Round 5:
Ch 4 (counts as 1 dc stitch + 1 stitch on rnd 5).
Work 3 dc, ch 2, 3 dc in the next ch-2 space of previous row - this is a corner. Ch 1.
Work (*1 dc - in every ch-1 space along the side, and 3 dc, ch 2, 3 dc) in the next ch-2 space - this is a corner.
Repeat from * around. End with a Ch 1. Join in the 3rd stitch of ch.
Repeat Round 5 until block measures 10".

55 - Blocks Stitch
Rows of Knitting
Knit:
Cast on 42 stitches.
Row 1: *K6, P6*. Repeat * to * ending K6.
Row 2: *P6, K6*. Repeat * to * ending P6.
Rows 3-6: Repeat Rows 1-2.
Row 7: Repeat Row 2.
Row 8: Repeat Row 1.
Rows 9-12: Repeat Row 7-8.
Repeat Rows 1-12 until block is 10".
Bind off.

56 - Granny Square '15'
Rounds of Crochet
Crochet:

Note: Use one color for all rounds.
Work the rounds the same as for Granny Square '1' on page 12.

57 - Granny Square '16'
Rounds of Crochet

Crochet:

Note: Use color 1 for rnd 1, color 2 for rnds 2 & 3, color 3 for rnds 4 & 5, color 4 for remaining rounds.

Begin: Ch 4, join with a sl st to form a ring.

Round 1: Ch 3 (counts as a dc)

Work yo, insert hook in ring, yo and pull through 1 loop, yo and pull through 2 loops.

Repeat one time. Yo and pull through the last 3 loops.

Work (*ch 2, Cluster Stitch). Repeat from * 6 times for a total of 8 'clusters'. Ch 2. Join with a sl st.

CLUSTER STITCH:

Work (*yo, insert hook in ring, yo and pull through 1 loop, yo and pull through 2 loops - keeping the last loop on the hook).

Round 2:

Ch 3 (counts as a dc). Turn.

Work 2 dc in the next ch-1.

Work (*3 dc, ch 2, 3 dc in the next ch-2 - this is a corner. Work 3 dc in each space between 'clusters' along the side.

Repeat from * for a total of 12 dc clusters. Join with a sl st.

Round 3:

Ch 3 (counts as 1 dc stitch on rnd 4). Turn.

Work (*1 dc - in every stitch along the side, and 3 dc, ch 2, 3 dc) in the next ch-2 space - this is a corner.

Repeat from * around. Join with a sl st.

Repeat Round 3 until block measures 10".

58 - Granny Square '17'
Rounds of Crochet

Crochet:

Note: Use color 1 for rnds 1, 2, 3, 4 & 5, and color 2 for remaining rounds.

Work the rounds the same as for Granny Square '1' on page 12.

59 - Dewdrops
Rows of Knitting

Knit:

Cast on 43 stitches.

Row 1: K2, work (P3, K3) across, ending P3, K2.

Row 2: P2, work (K3, P3) across, ending K3, P2.

Row 3: Repeat Row 1.

Row 4: K2, work (yo, sl 1, K2 together, pass slipped stitch over, yo, K3) across, ending yo, sl 1, K2 together, pass slipped stitch over, yo, K2.

Row 5: Repeat Row 2.

Row 6: Repeat Row 1.

Row 7: Repeat Row 2.

Row 8: K2 tog, work (yo, K3, yo, sl 1, K2 tog, pass slipped stitch over) across, ending yo, K3, yo, sl 1, K1, pass slipped stitch over.

Repeat Rows 1-8 until block is 10".

Bind off.

60 - Granny Square '18'
Rounds of Crochet

Crochet:

Note: Use color 1 for rnds 1, 2, 3, 4 & 5, and color 2 for remaining rounds.

Work the rounds the same as for Granny Square '1' on page 12.

61 - Blackberry Diamonds
Rows of Knitting

Knit:

Blackberry Stitch:
Work to the stitch where the berry is to be made. Knit into the front of the stitch, knit in back of stitch, knit in front of stitch to make 3 stitches on right needle. Slip the original stitch off left needle. Work (turn work, K3, turn work, P3) twice. Lift the berry stitches, in order, over the one nearest the point of the right needle, starting with the nearest one and working away from the needle point until only the first stitch remains on the needle.

Cast on 39 stitches.

Row 1: Knit.

Row 2 and all even-numbered rows: Purl.

Row 3: K5, Blackberry stitch*, K6, BS*.
Repeat * to * ending K5.

Row 5: K3, *BS, K1, BS, K1, BS, K9*. Repeat * to * ending BS, K1, BS, K1, BS, K3.

Row 7: (K1, BS) 5 times, (K2, BS) 2 times, (K1, BS) 5 times, (K2, BS) 2 times, (K1, BS) 5 times, K1.

Row 9: Repeat Row 5.

Row 11: Repeat Row 3.

Row 13: K12, BS, K13, BS, K12.

Row 14: Purl.

Repeat Rows 1-14 until block is 10".

Bind off.

62 - A Heart for You
Rows of Knitting and Duplicate Stitch

Knit:

Cast on 40 stitches.

Rows 1-4: Knit.

Row 5: K5, Purl across, K5.

Row 6: Knit.

Repeat
Rows 5 and 6 to within the last 4 rows.

Repeat Rows 1-4.

Bind off.

Heart: Add the heart with a 'Duplicate Stitch'. Use Red yarn and a large grosspoint needle.

63 - Granny Square '19'
Rounds of Crochet

Note: Use color 1 for rnd1, color 2 for rnd 2, color 1 for rnd 4, color 2 for rnd 4, color 1 for rnd 5, color 2 for rnd 6 and color 1 for remaining rounds.

Work the rounds the same as for Granny Square '1' on page 12.

see photos on page 27

Worsted weight yarn
for Knitting: Knitting needles size 10 or
for Crochet: Crochet hook size J/10 - 6mm

64 - Checkers
Rows of Knitting

Knit:

Cast on 40 stitches.

Row 1: *P2, K3*. Repeat across row.

Row 2: Knit.

Row 3: Repeat Row 1.

Row 4: Knit.

Row 5: Repeat Row 1.

Row 6: *P3, K2*. Repeat across row.

Row 7: Repeat Row 1.

Row 8: Repeat Row 6.

Row 9: Knit.

Row 10: Purl.

Row 11: Repeat Row 1

Row 12: Repeat Row 6.

Rows 13-16: Repeat Rows 1-4.

Repeat Rows 1-16 until block is 10".

Bind off.

65 - Single Crochet
Rows of Crochet

Crochet:

Begin: Ch 32.

Row 1: Sc in 2nd ch from hook. Work sc in each chain across the row. Turn.

Row 2: Ch 3. Sc in each stitch across. Ch 3. Turn.

Repeat Row 2 until block measures 10".

66 - Variety
Rows of Knitting

Knot Stitch:

(Bring yarn forward, take it over needle to the back, pass second stitch from right needle point over first stitch and made stitch.) 2 times

Cast on 40 stitches.

Row 1: *K2 (Knot st, K1) twice, Knot st*.
Repeat * to * across row.

continued

Row 2 and all even numbered rows: Purl.

Row 3: *K4, Knot st, K2, Knot st*. Repeat * to * across row.

Row 5: *K3, Knot st*. Repeat * to * across row.

Row 7: *K4, Knot st, K4*. Repeat * to * across row.

Row 9: *K2, Knot st, (K1, Knot st) twice*. Repeat * to * across row.

Repeat Rows 1-10 until block is 10".
Bind off.

67 - Plait Cable
Rows of Knitting

Knit:

Cast on 41 stitches.

TIP: Work an equal number of added stitches at either end of each row in established pattern. The center 13 stitches are used for the cable.

Row 1: K14, begin cable with P2, K9, P2, ending K14.

Row 2: P14, K2, P9, K2, P14.

Row 3: K14, P2, slip the next 3 sts onto a double pointed needle, leave in front, K3, K3 from dp needle, K3, P2, K14.

Row 4: Repeat Row 2.

Row 5: Repeat Row 1.

Row 6: Repeat Row 2.

Row 7: K14, P2, K3, sl 3 sts to dp needle, leave in back, K3, K3 from dp needle, P2, K14.

Row 8: Repeat Row 2.

Repeat Rows 1-8 until block is 10".
Bind off.

68 - Granny Square '20'
Rounds of Crochet

Crochet:

Note: Use color 1 for rnd 1, color 2 for rnds 2 & 3, color 3 for rnds 4 & 5, color 4 for remaining rounds.

Begin: Ch 4, join with a sl st to form a ring.

Round 1: Ch 3 (counts as a dc)

Work yo, insert hook in ring, yo and pull through 1 loop, yo and pull through 2 loops.

Repeat one time. Yo and pull through the last 3 loops.

Work (*ch 2, Cluster Stitch). Repeat from * 6 times for a total of 8 'clusters'. Ch 2. Join with a sl st.

CLUSTER STITCH:

Work (*yo, insert hook in ring, yo, pull through 1 loop, yo, pull through 2 loops).

Repeat from * 2 more times.
Yo and pull through the last 4 loops.)

Round 2:

Ch 3 (counts as a dc). Turn.

Work 2 dc in the next ch-1.

Work (*3 dc, ch 2, 3 dc in the next ch-2 - this is a corner. Work 3 dc in each space between 'clusters' along the side.

Repeat from * for a total of 12 dc clusters. Join with a sl st.

continued

Round 3:

Ch 3 (counts as 1 dc stitch on rnd 4). Turn.

Work (*1 dc - in every stitch along the side, and 3 dc, ch 2, 3 dc) in the next ch-2 space - this is a corner.

Repeat from * around. Join with a sl st.

Repeat Round 3 until block measures 10".

69 - Peppercorn
Rows of Knitting

Knit:

Peppercorn stitch: K1, P1, K1, P1, K1, P1 all into one stitch. Pull 6th stitch from needle end over. Pull 5 stitch over. Pull 4th stitch over. Pull 3rd stitch over. Pull 2nd stitch over.

Cast on 43 stitches.

Row 1: Purl (wrong side).

Row 2: P1, work (peppercorn stitch in next st, K4, P1) across.

Row 3: K1, work (P5, K1) across.

Row 4: P1, work (K2, peppercorn, K2, P1) across.

Row 5: Repeat Row 3.

Row 6: P1, work (K4, peppercorn, P1) across.

Row 7: Purl.

Repeat Rows 1-7 until block is 10".
Bind off.

70 - Half & Half
Rows of Knitting

Knit:

Cast on 40 stitches.

Row 1: Purl.

Row 2: P1, Knit across.

Row 3: Purl to last 2 sts, K2.

Row 4: P3, Knit across.

Repeat rows in the same manner, adding 1 stitch in stockinette stitch and losing 1 stitch in garter st pattern.

Knit last row.
Bind off.

71 - Wild Oats
Rows of Knitting

Knit:

Cast on 41 stitches.

Rows 1 and 5: Work (K2, slip 1 Purlwise, K1) across, ending K1.

Rows 2 and 6: P1, work (P1, slip 1 Purlwise, P2) across.

Row 3: Work (slip 2 sts onto cable needle, hold at back, K1, K2 sts from cable needle, K1) across, ending K1.

Rows 4 and 8: Purl.

Row 7: K1, work (K1, put the sl st on cable needle, hold at front, K2, knit st from cable needle) across.

Repeat Rows 1-8 until block is 10".
Bind off.

72 - Double Basket
Rows of Knitting

Knit:

Cast on 39 stitches.

Row 1: *P3, K3*. Repeat * to * ending P3.

Row 2: *K3, P3*. Repeat * to * ending K3.

Row 3: Repeat Row 1.

Row 4: Repeat Row 1.

Row 5: Repeat Row 2.

Row 6: Repeat Row 1.

Repeat Rows 1-6 until block is 10".
Bind off.

73 - Double Crochet
Rows of Crochet

Crochet:

Begin: Ch 34.

Row 1: Dc in 4th ch from hook. Dc in each chain across. Turn.

Row 2: Ch 3. Dc in each stitch across. Turn.

Repeat Row 2 until block measures 10".

74 - Wide Ribbing Rows
Rows of Knitting

Knit:

Cast on 40 stitches.

Row 1: *K4, P4*. Repeat across row.

Row 2: *P4, K4*. Repeat across row.

Repeat Rows 1 and 2 until block is 10".
Bind off.

75 - Soft Clusters
Rows of Knitting

Knit:

Cast on 40 stitches.

Row 1: Knit.

Row 2: P1, *yo, P2, pass yo over Purl stitches, P2*. Repeat * to * ending yo, P2, pass yo over Purl stitches, P1.

Row 3: Repeat Row 1.

Row 4: P3, *yo, P2, pass yo over Purl stitches, P2*. Repeat * to * ending P1.

Repeat Rows 1-4 until block is 10".
Bind off.

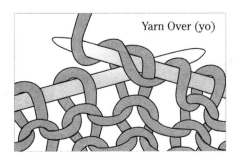

Yarn Over (yo)

Many Thanks to
Charlie Davis Young and Francis Berryhill
for carefully editing these instructions

How to Finish a Knit - Crochet Afghan

Once you have a variety of knit and crochet blocks, it is fun to assemble them together in a combination of 'mix and match' designs.

TIP: I like to choose a set of colors for my afghans, maybe a collection of 5 gold/greens, or 7 purples, or colors that look good together.

TIP: Scrappy Afghans look really good in any decor. Use leftovers from your yarn stash, or unravel yarn from outgrown sweaters for a personal touch.

TIP: If a block turns out a bit small (less than 10" x 10" after blocking), simply add 1 or 2 rows of dc binding around the block to make it large enough. See 'Bind the Edge' below.

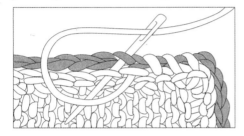

ASSEMBLY:

Assemble an Afghan by laying the blocks out on a work surface or table.

Join 5 to 7 completed squares into 6 to 8 vertical strips. Join the vertical strips together.

Lay out blocks in desired order. Join blocks as follows:

With right sides together, make a whip stitch with a yarn needle through the edge of the first square and the edge of the second square (see diagram).

Bring the needle around and insert it from right to left through the next loop on both squares. Continue in this manner, keeping the sewing yarn fairly loose.

BIND THE EDGE:

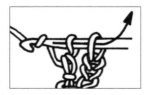

After the Afghan is assembled, make a finished edge to help the Afghan hold its shape, to make it a bit larger, and to give a finished appearance to your beautiful Afghan.

Sides: Using a Crochet hook J/10, pick up stitches around the edge. Pick up about 30 stitches on the side of each block.

Corners: At each corner, work 2 dc, ch 2, 2 dc - this rounds the corner.

Edging: Add 2 rows of double crochet (or add as many rows as desired).

Add additional rows if desired.

How to Finish Knit & Crochet Blocks

HOW TO BLOCK KNIT and CROCHET BLOCKS:

Due to the variety of pattern stitches used, the square blocks will benefit from being 'blocked' to the proper size (refer to pages 4 - 6).

Place each square (front side down) on a clean terry towel over a flat surface (each square should measure about 10" x 10"). Pin the block in place as needed using rust-proof pins.

Use a damp steam cloth. Steam lightly, allow to cool and dry completely.

How to Cut Fabric for Knitting

I like to cut my own fabric strips with a rotary cutter, that way I can get nice thin 1/4" strips that make knitting easy.

You'll need a rotary cutter with a sharp blade, a cutting mat and an acrylic cutting ruler.

I like to use continuous strips (this means with no knots).

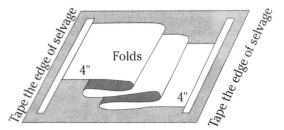

First fold cotton quilting fabric in large folds. The purpose of folding is to make the length you are cutting manageable, and so fabric will fit on a cutting mat.

Leave about 4" that is only 1 layer on each selvage edge. Make folds in the center area. Stagger the folds because it is difficult to cut 2 folds cleanly with a rotary cutter. Be sure the cutting edge is lined up.

Tape the edge of both selvages to the cutting mat with 1/2" masking tape. Mark masking tape every 1/4". Alternate your marks - one long mark and one short mark.

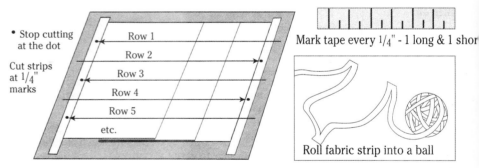

Mark tape every 1/4" - 1 long & 1 short

Roll fabric strip into a ball

Cut the fabric into a <u>continuous strip</u>. Look at the diagram carefully.

← **Row 1:** Cut through selvage on the <u>right</u>, stop 1/4" from selvage edge on the <u>left</u>.
→ **Row 2:** Cut through selvage on the <u>left</u>, stop 1/4" from selvage edge on the <u>right</u>. Repeat Rows 1 and 2 until you reach the end of the fabric.

Remove the tape from each section. Beginning at one end, roll fabric strip into a ball. If any strips were accidently cut through at the selvage, simply tie a small knot.

How to Finish a Quilt

These quilts have a wonderful handmade look and lots of texture and color variation.

"Block" your knit or crochet squares to 10" x 10", and iron interfacing to the back of each square (refer to pages 4 - 6).

Lay out blocks in desired order. Join blocks along the edges with a sewing machine (it should sew through fabric as well as squares that are Knit or Crochet).

Sew blocks with right sides together, and shift the corners just a bit if they are too bulky. Layer the finished top, cotton quilt batting and backing fabric. Quilt the layers together. Quilt right through the layers of the Knit blocks and fabric blocks, or simply leave the Knit blocks without quilting.

To finish, sew a binding around the edge.

Le experienced great sadness for many days. On one particularly difficult day, she and her husband were driving through Valley Oaks Ranch where they had previously lived, and saw that one of the few remaining homes in the area had been put up for sale.

They immediately bought it and began the process of making some changes to suit them. During that time, she came into our store and purchased upholstery fabric for an old chair that had been given to her. When we received our squares, there were stitched squares in just the colors she had picked for her new home, and we saved it for her.

Vickie happened to come into the store after all the blankets were done. We gave a special blanket to her and she was just overwhelmed and pleased with how well the colors would match her new home. She walked around the store, hugging her blanket the entire time.

see stitch instructions on page 12

Make 35 Blocks to 'mix and match' for this beautiful afghan blanket. Bind around the edges with yarn (page 18).

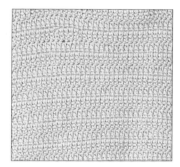

14 - Triple Crochet
Rows of Crochet

17 - Granny Square '2'
Rounds of Crochet

15 - Granny Square '1'
Rounds of Crochet

18 - Twisted Rib
Rows of Knitting

20 - Moss Ribbing
Rows of Knitting

22 - Triple Crochet
Rows of Crochet

16 - Seed Stitch Diamonds
Rows of Knitting

19 - Double Crochet
Rows of Crochet

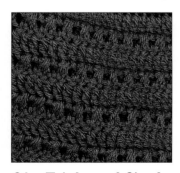

21 - Triple and Single
Rows of Crochet

23 - Stockinette Stitch with Homespun Yarn
Rows of Knitting

Goldenrod Afghan

Knit and Crochet Blocks with Yarn

Individual Stories:

The individual stories of fire victims are truly touching.

Colleen, a well-respected local artist, lost her home and all of her knitting materials collected over many years. She spent hours in our store trying to document and recreate that collection. At the time, she said she wanted to knit her own blanket. When she later saw a very beautiful one that had been donated, she said, "Well, that would fit in my home, I love it!"

And, yes, it is now in her rental home waiting for her new house to be built.

see stitch instructions on page 13

24 - Double Crochet
Rows of Crochet

28 - Triple Crochet
Rows of Crochet

Make 35 Blocks to 'mix and match' for this beautiful afghan blanket. Bind around the edges with yarn (page 18).

25 - Quaker Variation
Rows of Knitting

29 - Diamonds for You
Rows of Knitting

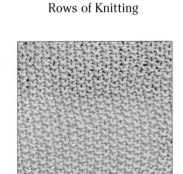

26 - Seed Stitch
Rows of Knitting

30 - Granny Square '3'
Rounds of Crochet

32 - Dancing Dots
Rows of Knitting

34 - Variation Stitch
Rows of Knitting

27 - Wide Welts
Rows of Knitting

31 - Triple Sets
Rows of Crochet

33 - Welt Variation
Rows of Knitting

35 - Big Welt Stitch
Rows of Knitting

Nature's Garden

Knit and Crochet Blocks with Yarn

We made masculine-colored blankets for two elderly men who were fire victims. Dennis is one of these brave men, a retired fire fighter, who did not evacuate, but rather, he stayed to help save neighbors' homes. Unfortunately, his own home was not spared…he lost everything!

Wayne, the other gentleman that received a masculine-style blanket, was very appreciative! He evacuated from his home and lived in his car during the fires. His wife lives in a convalescent home, so he and his dog parked in the parking lot to be near her. Sadly, his home was a total loss, so receiving a beautiful, handmade blanket was a true comfort to him!

see stitch instructions on page 14

36 - Granny Square '4'
Rounds of Crochet

40 - Framed Square
Rows of Crochet

37 - Granny Square '5'
Rounds of Crochet

41 - Garter Ribs
Rows of Knitting

Make 42 Blocks to 'mix and match' for this beautiful afghan blanket. Bind around the edges with yarn (page 18).

38 - Big Ripple Stitch
Rows of Crochet

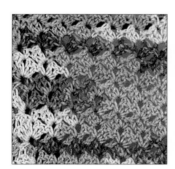

42 - Shells
Rows of Crochet

44 - Granny Square '8'
Rounds of Crochet

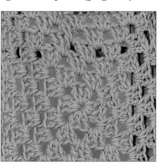

46 - Granny Square '10'
Rounds of Crochet

39 - Granny Square '6'
Rounds of Crochet

43 - Granny Square '7'
Rounds of Crochet

45 - Granny Square '9'
Rounds of Crochet

47 - Cluster Shells
Rows of Crochet

see stitch instructions on pages 15 - 16

Make 35 Blocks to 'mix and match' for these beautiful afghan blankets. Bind around the edges with yarn (page 18).

48 - Granny Square '11'
Rounds of Crochet

52 - Granny Square '13'
Rounds of Crochet

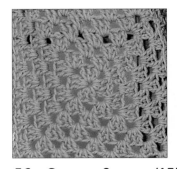

56 - Granny Square '15'
Rounds of Crochet

60 - Granny Square '18'
Rounds of Crochet

49 - Single Crochet
Rows of Crochet

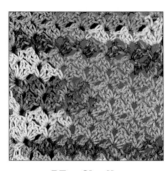

53 - Shells
Rows of Knitting

57 - Granny Square '16'
Rounds of Crochet

61 - Blackberry Diamonds
Rows of Knitting

50 - Granny Square '12'
Rounds of Crochet

54 - Granny Square '14'
Rounds of Crochet

58 - Granny Square '17'
Rounds of Crochet

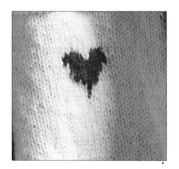

62 - A Heart for You
Rows of Knitting
and Duplicate Stitch

51 - Giant Welts
Rows of Knitting

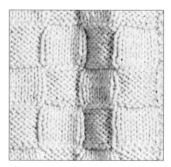

55 - Blocks Stitch
Rows of Knitting

59 - Dewdrops
Rows of Knitting

63 - Granny Square '19'
Rounds of Crochet

One square that Janell, a knit instructor, made for the project was a white square with a red heart stitched in the center. That one square was my inspiration for the red, white, and blue blanket that we gave to our local firehouse. These courageous firefighters saved so many of our homes and endured long, hard work for days in doing so. Ironically, while they were out saving our homes, much of their own fire department property was burned. I can still remember seeing the photo in our local paper of the fire department's white fencing that was all burned, twisted, and warped, and their fire department sign, half of which was charcoal black while the other half was fine.

Our hope is that their "blanket of love" can be used on one of their trucks to bring comfort to someone experiencing a future tragedy.

Red, White and Bold

Knit and Crochet Blocks with Yarn

Spirits of the Earth

Knit and Crochet Blocks with Yarn

Nan and her husband received an "Autumn Colors" blanket from our project to enhance the remains of their adobe-style home. They both are in their eighties and lost almost everything in this fire! All 12 acres of their fruit producing groves, the trailers their workers were housed in, and a large workshop filled with a lifetime of Fallbrook memorabilia and vehicles were lost!

Their home endured much smoke damage, but because it was built with true adobe brick it endured. Of course, all the windows exploded out, but thankfully, they were some of the lucky fire victims who at least had a structure to return to.

Needless to say, they were so appreciative of the blanket they received!